SIMPLE MACHINE PROJECTS

Making Machines with Pulleys

Chris Oxlade

heinemann
raintree

© 2015 Raintree
an imprint of Capstone Global Library, LLC
Chicago, Illinois

To contact Capstone Global Library, please call 800-747-4992,
or visit our web site www.capstonepub.com

Edited by James Benefield and Erika Shores
Designed by Steve Mead
Original illustrations © Capstone Global Library Ltd 2015
Picture research by Jo Miller
Production by Victoria Fitzgerald
Originated by Capstone Global Library Ltd
Printed and bound in China by Leo Paper Group

18 17 16 15 14
10 9 8 7 6 5 4 3 2 1

Library of Congress Cataloging-in-Publication Data
Oxlade, Chris, author.
  Making machines with pulleys / Chris Oxlade.
      pages cm.—(Simple machine projects)
ISBN 978-1-4109-6800-5 (hb)—ISBN 978-1-4109-6807-4
(pb)—ISBN 978-1-4109-6821-0 (ebook) 1. Pulleys—Juvenile
literature. 2. Simple machines—Juvenile literature. I. Title.

  TJ1103.O85 2015
  621.8'11—dc23   2014013707

**This book has been officially leveled by using the F&P Text
Level Gradient™ Leveling System.**

Acknowledgments
We would like to thank the following for permission to repro-
duce photographs:

All photos Capstone Studio: Karon Dubke except: Alamy: M
Itani, 29 (bottom); Newscom: Design Pics, 18, Getty Images/
AFP/Justin Tallis, 29 (top), Peter & Georgina Bowater Stock
Connection Worldwide, 26; Shutterstock: fotum, 21, Narong-
sak, 5, peresanz, 19, Steve Norman, 13, TFoxFoto, 20, Yarygin,
27; Superstock: Science Faction/Ed Darack, 7.

Design Elements: Shutterstock: Timo Kohlbacher.

We would like to thank Harold Pratt and Richard Taylor for
their invaluable help in the preparation of this book.

CONTENTS

Some words are shown in bold, **like this**. You can find out what they mean by looking in the glossary.

WHAT IS A PULLEY?

Have you ever raised a flag up a flagpole by pulling a rope? Or have you adjusted the sails on a sailboat? If you have, pulleys will have helped you, because flagpoles and sailboats have pulleys that help them to work.

A pulley is a simple machine (see below for more information about simple machines). In this book, you'll see many examples of pulleys. The projects to try will also help you to understand how different kinds of pulley work.

SIMPLE MACHINES

Pulleys are one of the five types of simple machines. The other four are the **lever**, the **wheel and axle**, the **ramp** (and the **wedge**), and the **screw**. Also, **springs** are like simple machines. Simple machines help us to do jobs such as lifting or moving heavy loads, pulling things, and gripping things tightly.

Pulleys around us

Sometimes you have to look hard to find pulleys, because not that many machines use them. At home, you might see them in window blinds and some garden tools. Outdoors, you can see them on construction cranes and on ships and boats.

 These pulleys are at the top of the boom of a construction crane.

HOW PULLEYS WORK

A pulley is made up of a pulley wheel with a rope around it. The wheel normally has a groove around the rim that stops the rope from sliding off the wheel. The simplest pulley system has just one pulley wheel with a rope around it. It changes the direction of your pull.

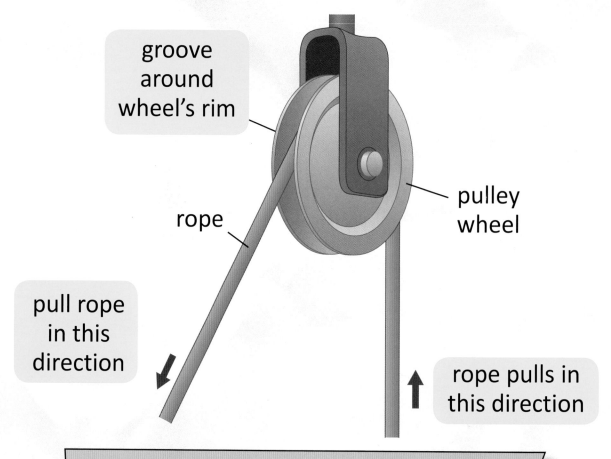

groove around wheel's rim

rope

pulley wheel

pull rope in this direction

rope pulls in this direction

This diagram shows the parts of a pulley and how it changes the direction of a force.

Lifting with pulleys

A simple pulley system makes it easier to lift things. Builders use simple pulleys to lift materials up **scaffolding**. Some water wells have a simple pulley to lift buckets full of water.

pulley wheel

When you pull the rope downward, the rope pulls the bucket of water upward.

FORCE AND MOTION

Simple machines, such as pulleys, can change **force** and motion (movement). A simple machine can make a force (a push or a pull) larger or smaller, or change its direction. A simple machine can also make a motion larger or smaller, or change its direction.

A Simple Pulley

In this project, you'll make a pulley wheel. Simple pulleys change directions of force. They make lifting weights easier.

1 Measure 1 in. (3 cm) up from the bottom of the toilet paper tube. With strong scissors, cut across the tube. You will be left with a shallow ring.

What you need:
- a cardboard toilet paper tube
- a ruler
- strong scissors
- two old CDs or DVDs (ask an adult to make sure you can use these)
- all-purpose glue
- a pencil
- string
- a small weight such as a battery or an eraser

STEP 1

2 Put glue around one edge of the cardboard tube, as shown in the picture.

STEP 2

3 Put the CD on your work surface and put the tube on top of it, with the glued side facing down, as shown in the picture. Make sure that the center of the tube lines up with the center of the CD.

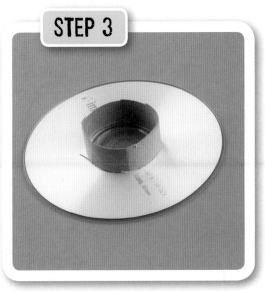

STEP 3

4 Glue the second CD to the other side of the tube to complete the pulley wheel, as shown (right). Again, make sure that the center of the CD lines up with the center of the tube. Allow the glue to dry for a few minutes.

STEP 4

5 Now you will need some help. Slide the pencil through the hole in the center of the pulley wheel (see picture). Ask your helper to hold the ends of the pencil at head height.

STEP 5

6 Put your chosen weight (for example, an eraser) on the floor and loop the string over the pulley.

7 Pull down on the end of the string to lift the weight. Watch what happens to the pulley wheel.

STEP 7

8 You can try lifting the weight by pulling the string **horizontally** instead of downward (see below).

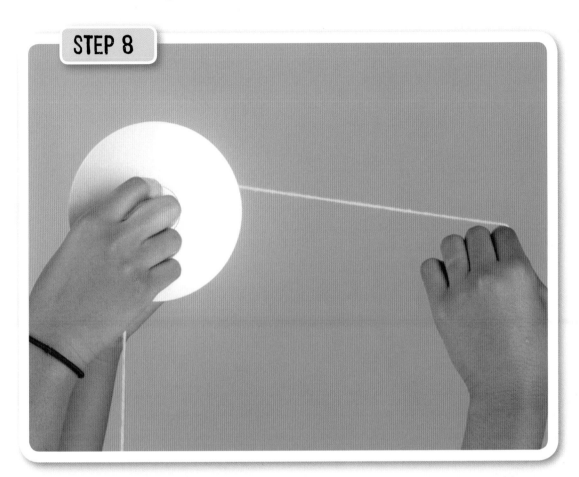

STEP 8

What did you find out?

A simple pulley system changes the direction of a force. You pulled down on the string, and the string pulled up on the weight. The pulley also changed a horizontal pull into a **vertical** pull. You pulled on the string horizontally, and the string pulled upward on the weight.

COMPOUND PULLEYS

A pulley system with two or more pulley wheels is called a compound pulley system. A system with two pulley wheels doubles the strength of the pull you make. That way, the force you need to lift an object is half the weight of the object.

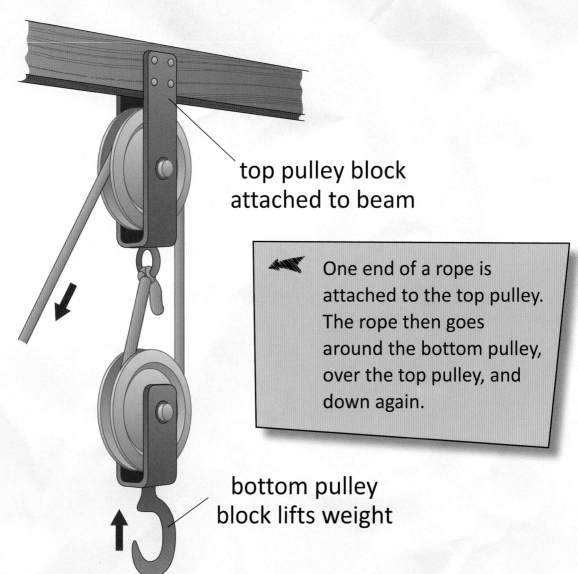

top pulley block attached to beam

One end of a rope is attached to the top pulley. The rope then goes around the bottom pulley, over the top pulley, and down again.

bottom pulley block lifts weight

Adding more pulleys

Each extra pulley increases the size of the pull you make. For example, if you have four pulley wheels (two at the top and two at the bottom), the system makes your pull four times as big.

This sort of compound pulley is also called a **block and tackle**.

SUPER STRENGTH

A compound pulley system can make a force much, much larger. Using a pulley system with 20 pulley wheels (10 at the top and 10 at the bottom), you could lift a car on your own!

A Compound Pulley System

This is a project to make a compound pulley system. Remember that this is a pulley system that increases a force, making it easier to lift heavier objects.

1 Make two pulley wheels using the instructions on pages 8–11.

What you need:
- four old CDs or DVDs (ask an adult to make sure you can use these)
- a short, strong cardboard tube (such as the cardboard ring from sticky tape)
- small object for a weight (such as a battery)
- all-purpose glue
- a round-sided pencil
- string

2 Cut a 3-ft.- (1-m-) long piece of string. At each end, double over the last 4 in. (10 cm) of string, then tie an overhand knot (see page 31) to make a loop.

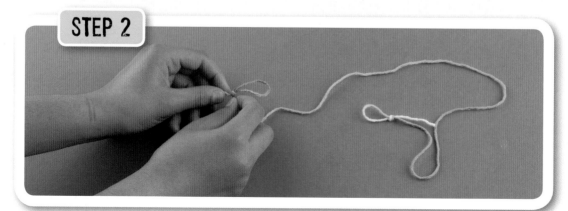

STEP 2

3 Thread the string through the center of one of your pulleys (see picture). This will be the bottom pulley in your compound pulley system.

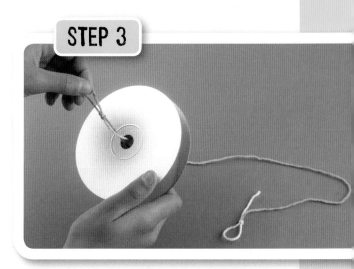

4 Cut a piece of string 20 in. (50 cm) long. Tie one end of this string to both the loops on the string that is through the hole in the bottom pulley. Tie or tape the small weight to the other end (see picture).

STEP 4

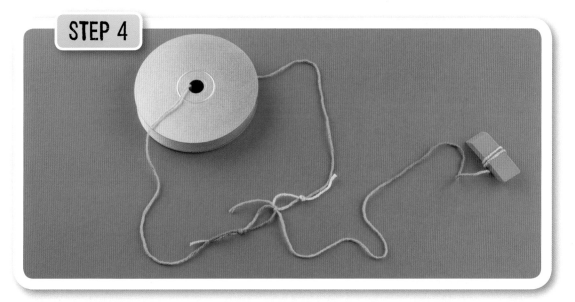

5 Put the round-sided pencil through the other pulley wheel. The wheel should spin freely around the pencil. This wheel will be the top pulley wheel in your pulley system.

6 Cut a piece of string about 6½ ft. (2 m) long. As in step 2, double over the last 4 inches at one end of the string and tie an overhand knot to make a loop. Put the loop over the pencil, against one side of the pulley.

STEP 6

7 You need some help for the next step. Ask your helper to hold the top pulley (the one with the pencil through it). See the picture below.

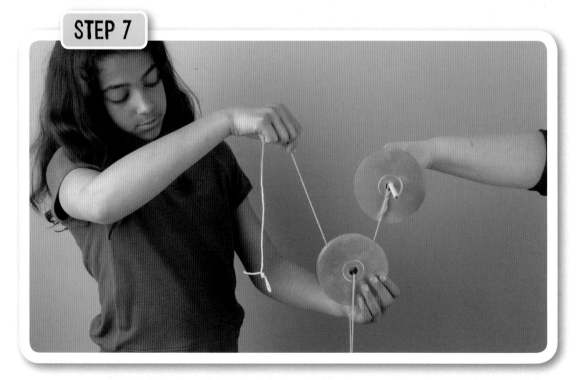

STEP 7

8 Hold the bottom pulley below the top pulley. Feed the end of the string from the top pulley around the bottom pulley, and back up and over the top pulley.

9 Now you can lift the weight. Pull down on the loose end of the string (see below). Watch what happens.

STEP 9

What did you find out?

Compare how hard it was to lift the weight with and without the pulley system. You should find that the pulley system makes it easier to lift the weight on the end of the string.

PULLEYS IN HISTORY

We don't know who invented the pulley. It must have been invented thousands of years ago. We know this because there are pictures of pulleys being used in ancient Greece and ancient Rome.

Simple machines such as pulleys were the only way to make the large forces needed for lifting, moving, and shaping materials. Pulleys were part of the enormous construction machines that Greeks and Romans relied on to build their great buildings and bridges.

 This drawing shows a pulley wheel in use on a hoisting machine, hundreds of years ago.

Ship's pulleys

Pulley systems have been part of the rigging on sailing ships for thousands of years. Sailors used a block and tackle to adjust the angle of heavy sails. This took the best advantage of the wind. The largest sailing ships needed hundreds of blocks and tackles altogether.

This is a block (part of a block and tackle) on an old sailing ship.

ARCHIMEDES'S PULLEY?

It's possible that the famous Greek mathematician Archimedes invented the compound pulley (see page 12 to remind yourself about compound pulleys).

PULLEY BELTS

So far, we've seen how pulley wheels are used in simple and compound pulley systems for changing forces. Pulley wheels are also used to transfer movement from one place to another.

This is done with a loop of rope or rubber called a pulley belt. The belt is looped around two wheels, so when you turn one wheel, the other wheel turns, too. Using pulley wheels of different sizes, you can make one wheel turn faster than the other.

A pulley belt links a large pulley wheel to a small pulley wheel.

Using chains

Chains are often used instead of belts to transfer movement. Cogs are used instead of pulley wheels. The teeth on the cogs interlock with the holes in the chain. This makes sure the chain doesn't slip on the cogs. If you have a bicycle, you can see a chain and cogs at work.

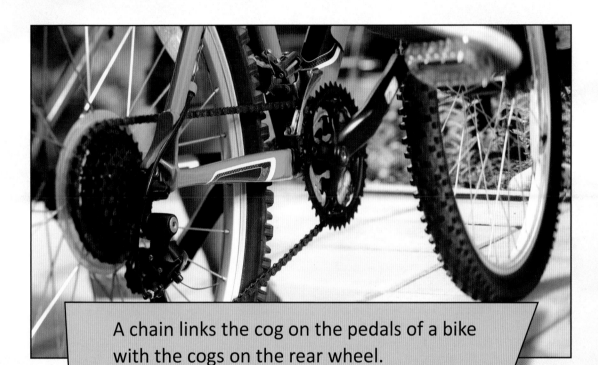

A chain links the cog on the pedals of a bike with the cogs on the rear wheel.

SKI LIFT PULLEYS

Ski lifts and cable cars rely on pulleys. The gondolas (or chairs) are attached to a giant loop of steel cable that goes around huge pulleys at the bottom and top of the lift.

Making a Pulley Belt

In this project, you can see how a pulley belt transfers movement from one place to another, and also how it can change the speed of movement.

1 Cut off the lid or the flaps of your box.

2 Make a pencil mark on each side of the box, 1 in. (2 cm) from the end and about an inch down from the top.

STEP 2

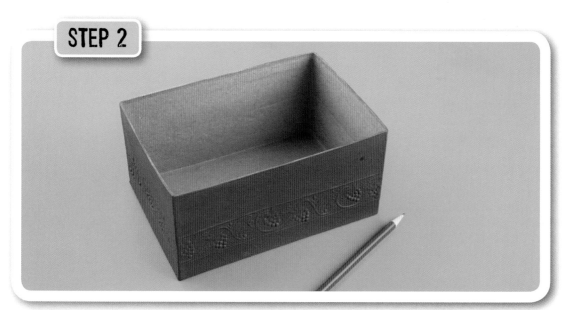

3 Carefully pierce the box with a sharp pencil at both the marks.

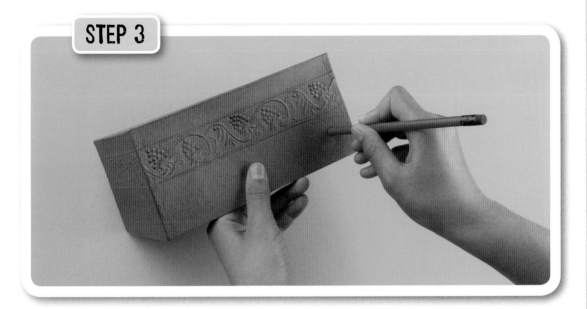

STEP 3

4 Wiggle the pencil around to make the holes a little larger. The pencil should spin freely in the holes.

STEP 5

5 Put the pencil through the holes to make an axle, trapping a rubber band, as shown (right).

6 Pull the band gently along the inside of the box, so it stretches a little, as shown. Make a mark on both sides of the box level with the end of the band.

STEP 6

7 Pierce holes at the marks in step 6 and widen them, as before.

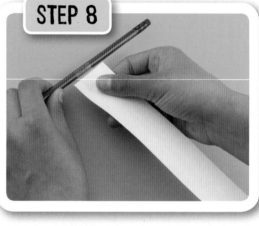

STEP 8

8 Cut a piece of thin cardboard about 1½ x 8 in. (4 x 20 cm). Tape one end of the cardboard to the center of one of the pencils.

9 Wrap the cardboard tightly around the pencil to make a pulley wheel. Put tape around the cardboard to keep it from unwinding.

STEP 9

10 Make sure the holes are big enough for the pencil with the cardboard around it to fit. Put the pencil back through the box, this time with the rubber band around the completed pulley wheel.

11 Turn the pencil with the cardboard on it and watch what happens to the other pencil.

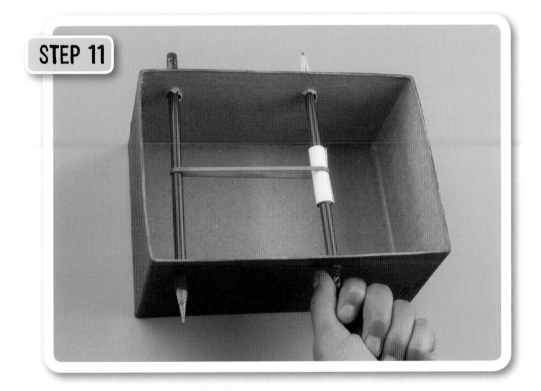

STEP 11

What did you find out?
In this project, the band worked as a pulley belt, and the pencils worked as pulley wheels. The pencil with no cardboard around it turned faster.

PULLEYS IN COMPLEX MACHINES

Many complicated machines contain simple machines such as pulley wheels, pulley belts, cogs, and chains.

Compound pulleys

Machines that lift very heavy objects contain compound pulleys. The most common example is a construction crane. Large cranes have compound pulleys with many pulley wheels. A hook connected to the bottom set of wheels lifts heavy objects such as buckets of concrete.

Pulleys work on a giant mechanical excavator at a mine.

Car and motorcycle engines have pulley belts that transfer movement from one part of the engine to another. On motorcycles, a chain between the engine and the rear wheel turns the wheel to make the motorcycle move along the road.

A motorcycle's engine pulls on a flexible chain around a cog on the rear wheel.

PULLEYS, WHEELS, AND AXLES

On a bicycle, the pedals and front cog are a wheel and axle, which is another simple machine. Turning the pedals pulls the chain, which turns the rear wheel, so the wheel and axles and pulley work together.

FACTS AND FUN

AMAZING PULLEYS

The largest sailing ships, such as clippers and galleons, need hundreds of sets of blocks and tackles to raise and control their many huge sails.

Archimedes (see page 19) designed and used a pulley. Using it, he could move a fully loaded ship that was stuck on the shore on his own!

The SSCV Thialf is one the world's largest floating cranes. The pulley block attached to its hook contains around 40 pulley wheels.

The first bicycle to have a chain was the Rover Safety Bicycle of 1885, designed by the English inventor John Starley.

The world's longest conveyor is a staggering 22 miles (35 kilometers) long. It carries crushed limestone rock from a quarry in India to a factory in Bangladesh.

PULLEYS TODAY

All simple machines, including pulleys, were invented thousands of years ago. The pulley was invented at least 2,000 years ago. Some jobs that pulleys did in the past are now done by powered machines, but pulleys still do some jobs that they have done for hundreds of years. The pulley will be useful for years to come.

Where and what are these pulleys?

Research more about pulleys on boats.

Where could a pulley be in the supermarket?

GLOSSARY

block and tackle compound pulley with a block at each end, each containing one or more pulleys

horizontal parallel with the ground. A plank is horizontal when one end is at the same height as the other end.

lever long bar that is pushed or pulled against a fulcrum to help move heavy loads or cut material

ramp simple machine used to lift heavy objects

scaffolding temporary structure of poles and planks that builders put up to reach the outside of a building

screw simple machine that has a spiral-shaped thread, used to attach or lift materials

spring device that can be pressed or pulled but returns to its first shape when released

vertical at right angles to the ground (for example, a plank is vertical when one end is directly above the other end)

wedge simple machine used to split apart materials

wheel and axle simple machine made up of a wheel on an axle, used to turn or lift objects

FIND OUT MORE

Books

Deane-Pratt, Ade. *Simple Machines* (How Things Work). New York: PowerKids, 2012.

Oxlade, Chris. *Pulleys* (Simple Machines). North Mankato, Minn.: Smart Apple Media, 2008.

Walker, Sally M., and Roseann Feldmann. *Put Pulleys to the Test* (How Do Simple Machines Work?). Minneapolis: Lerner, 2012.

Web sites

Facthound offers a safe, fun way to find Internet sites related to this book. All of the sites on Facthound have been researched by our staff.

Here's all you do:
Visit *www.facthound.com*
Type in this code: 9781410968005

INDEX